Business Development Practices, Programs and Strategies
Preparation and Planning for Sustainable Prosperity

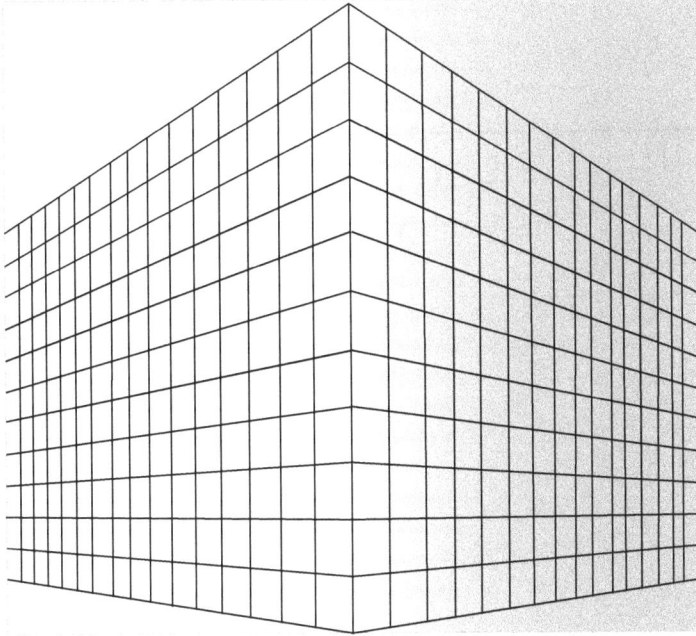

A Defining Moment

The Advent of Sustainable Prosperity

Fundamental Operational Thinking
Overview and Introduction

T. Lewis Company

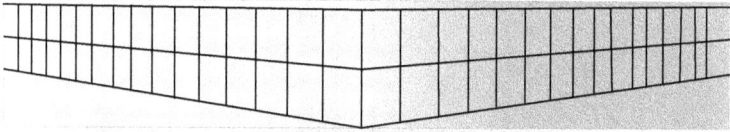

"Operational thinking that is largely governed by 'outwardly focused' steering influences...

...providing practical realism – 'common business sense' – in functional interpretations at all levels."

The Value of "Extrinsic Reasoning" as an Approach to Fundamental Operational Thinking

A Concept for Organizational Development

Overview and Introduction

Basics of the Concept
2nd Edition

T. Lewis Company, LLC

www.tlewiscompany.com
resources@tlewiscompany.com

A Defining Moment

The Advent of Sustainable Prosperity

Contents

Prologue...

Sustainable Prosperity

Sustainable prosperity must, of course, be woven into the fabric of every operational setting.

Still, though often mistakenly presumed, it always seems a bit unnerving to contemplate... and difficult to assess... especially when pressed to navigate a weakened economy or to prevail in an increasingly competitive marketplace.

Or to pursue a meaningful transformation.

Not remarkably...

- There might be urgent pressure to rise to a new level, amidst a variety of functional weaknesses or negative tendencies.

  Along with a dreary history of expensive, out-sourced improvement programs that have proven futile, or "text-book" enhancement methods that have failed.

- Or perhaps there is a mandate to create a better work environment.

  A safe, ecologically sound workplace.

And a fit, informed workforce with a dutiful regard for safety and the natural environment.

A securely compliant yet business-sensible operational framework that inspires sound internal choices, and is thus not forced to withstand unexpected... often debilitating... corrective stipulations imposed by others.

One that is enhanced rather than inhibited by associated obligations.

- There might be a pledge to preserve a sound heritage in the midst of delicate succession planning or a difficult transition.

- Or merely an attempt to fulfill a vision or pursue an ideal.

Doubtless there are many others.

Yet all reflect complexities that can be put in order by an engaging form of thought.

One that rouses a self-regulating undercurrent that will *safeguard* sustainable prosperity.

"...a self-regulating undercurrent that will safeguard sustainable prosperity."

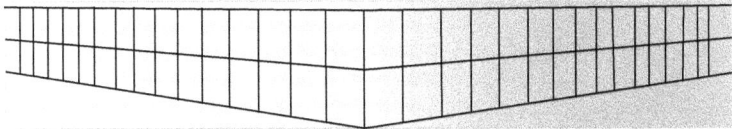

Chapter 1.

The Turning Point

Each of these cases could... or, more likely, *should*... trigger a "pivotal revelation" in operational awareness.

A turning point.

Some might relate to *systemic weaknesses*.

Shortcomings that have held less significance in the past, were cast a blind eye, or were viewed from a biased or unknowing perspective:

- Lapses in operational foresight that have become increasingly apparent.

- Unpleasant friction in ongoing strategic initiatives or succession schemes.

- A frustratingly unfulfilled vision that has always seemed so clearly obtainable.

- Willful resistance to change.

Allowing reasonably lenient remedial time frames, and greater tolerance of incidental factors.

Others, in contrast, relate to rather *sudden breaches*.

Crippling, ill-timed disruptions... commonly intense or "fiery":

- A severe functional setback, failure or penalty.

- A serious operational incident, succession clash, or a bitter break of trust.

Requiring quick and focused responses.

Adjustments predictably cope with confrontation and false impressions as well, adding to the problems.

Still further, not only are these matters rather tortuous, ensuing decisions often bear fateful results.

Searching for relief, many "campaigners" seek outside advice from capable specialists, but find it difficult to link these products or services with internal aspirations and cultures.

Core factors are thus wrongly assumed, misunderstood or ignored, and subsequent courses of action are impractical and counterproductive.

Clearly artificial and forced, internal participants become immediately distrustful... friction overpowers collaboration.

And developmental planning proves maddening, time after time.

Persuasive schemes come from conscientious "in-house" contributors as well, yet they, too, can suffer limited success or failure for similar reasons.

Avoiding "outside help" or fallible internal programs by dodging or discouraging them might handily reduce adverse cost and friction.

Then again, it might also thwart a "brighter" future.

Of course... the future might be richly promising for some, with no menacing issues at hand.

For others, however, the brightness is fading and functional limitations have become painfully obvious.

Crucial opportunities exceed capabilities; even minor complications seem to overwhelm organizational know-how.

And "solutions" must favorably affect functional behavior throughout the *entire* operating environment.

A formidable task.

Nevertheless, there *is* a sure "first step"... a simple form of *operational thinking* that will embrace *every* functional setting.

A basic tool that will maximize workplace efficiency and creativity, facilitate effective developmental programs, and elevate health, safety and environmental interests.

All within a business-sensible context.

And it works.

Initiatives will be properly tailored and launched in receptive surroundings; implementation time frames will be shortened, costs reduced and friction minimized.

There will be comfortable candor in decision-making, a confident outlook and a positive mindset; an energizing operational climate that will strengthen every function, spawning success and security that might have previously been unimaginable.

Urgent complexity will transition to functional clarity; critical events and decision-making will occur as planned components of well-founded comprehensive strategies.

Operational improvements and self-regulation practices will "pop up" naturally with sound footing and within a common frame of reference.

Unknown talents will come forth; creativity will flourish, all with respect for the common good.

A genuine "reawakening".

That being so, the *real* need does not lie in "useful" responses to specific difficulties as they arise, it rests deeper in the operating culture and transcends those points in time.

And it is *best* approached by advocating a universal practice of selflessly *enhancing positive functional traits and disposing of negative ones.*

One that will produce an operating culture in which complex issues are comfortably engaged, in an orderly manner, and cooperatively resolved.

And one in which the best fitting strategies, programs and service providers are properly assessed, selected and put in place.

It calls for the introduction of a simple dynamic... a basic method of interpretation that can be called *"extrinsic reasoning".*

The gateway to sustainable prosperity.

A Defining Moment.

Key Definitions and Terminology -

Certain expressions require a precise definition of common words or phrases. It is important that the intention is clear in each case.

Extrinsic Reasoning

The word *extrinsic* is used to represent piloting influences that come from "without" or from the "outside"; measures of value that are external to an operation, task assignment or individual participant.

And *reasoning* is an adaptation of the expression "sensory processing"; the assessment of operating characteristics in accordance with a "mental model"... an individual's perception of suitability that has been shaped through training, experience or persuasion.

Observational comprehension and the nature of decisions regarding operational elements are governed by this interpretive mechanism.

Hence the term *extrinsic reasoning* merely implies a broadening of this mental model... a shift in perception to accommodate a more complete definition of suitability. One that supportively acknowledges "outwardly focused" steering influences.

Extrinsic reasoning encourages all individuals to:

- Determine the true "identity" of an operating environment.

- Offer suggestions, developmental programs and strategic initiatives that are rational, constructive and fruitful.

- Quietly counsel against non-cooperative tendencies that

selfishly reject, disregard, or block the acceptance of sound enhancement methods and improvement schemes.

By applying practical realism to operational interpretations.

The true "first step".

Intrinsic Behavior

The term *intrinsic behavior* is used to personify "inwardly focused" thinking; thoughts that cater to the basic, self-important nature of an individual and that tend to hide or manipulate vital aspects of an operation for personal gain. Actual needs are then impeded or frustrated.

It is typically characterized by a detached decision-making mindset that is artificially committed to a rigid "internal" focus or agenda.

At times attributable to instinctive "bottom line thinking", intrinsic behavior is often unknowing or unintentional.

Receptive Capacity

The willingness, means and proficiency of individuals or functional alliances within an operating environment to understand, endorse and pursue operational initiatives.

Sustainable Prosperity

A fluid, responsive and non-presumptuous journey through a limitless battleground of operational influences.

A progression shaped by the underlying potency of sound core principles... fundamental values that have been derived through *extrinsic reasoning*.

"Certain expressions require a precise definition of common words or phrases."

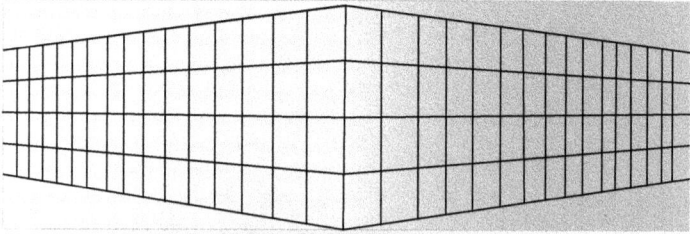

"Urgent complexity will transition to functional clarity..."

Chapter 2.

A Battleground of Operational Influences

Professionally, we often encounter *intrinsic behavior.*

And we each, almost without doubt, have exhibited this trait as well.

Driven by ego, self-indulgence or indifference; insecurity, apprehension, anxiety and such, the propensity appears in many forms and all operational settings.

Though perhaps inadvertent and commonly ascribed to ordinary human nature, the operational influence can nonetheless be among the most detrimental.

But this damaging influence can be "battled" and reversed through *extrinsic reasoning,* an all-inclusive practice that gives vital and transparent simplicity to complex issues.

An outwardly focused interpretive mechanism that will empower individuals at all levels to identify and quietly confront the harmful influences of *intrinsic behavior.*

Favorable aspects of the operating environment will be spontaneously enhanced... and negative ones diminished... with less tension, always reinforcing the common good.

And producing higher, perhaps previously unimaginable, levels of success.

Outside service providers will be properly integrated and ex-pected to hold an unprompted respect for in-house sensibility, operational awareness and technical expertise. They will not be permitted to hastily judge the values of in-place programs, practices or operational expectations.

Nor will they be free to abruptly dictate corrective measures for what appear to be "typical" operational shortcomings.

Levels of participation and collaborative processes will instead be internally pre-determined and capably monitored throughout the term of involvement.

Extrinsic reasoning is the fundamental line of defense against harmful operational influences.

An *outwardly focused* "lifeblood" that will offer secure passage through a thorny battleground.

"...producing higher, perhaps previously unimaginable, levels of success."

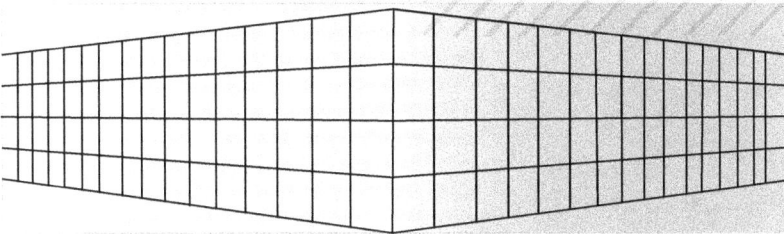

Chapter 3.

A Simple Concept

Extrinsic reasoning.

Unpretentious and balanced operational thinking.

Whereby fundamental values are measured in *outwardly focused* terms, with key regulating principles derived from *external* strategic or functional traits.

An essential practice that brings about a feeling of *realism*.

Instilling confidence that an operation, function or participant will be *wisely* positioned when common sense prevails.

———

Everyday experiences, though, suggest that "extrinsic thought" is often considered flawed and strikingly contrary to bottom line interests.

Instinctively rejected as a consequence, operational ambitions are frequently rooted in "intrinsic soil".

Picture the story line of any broad or focused, internal or exter-

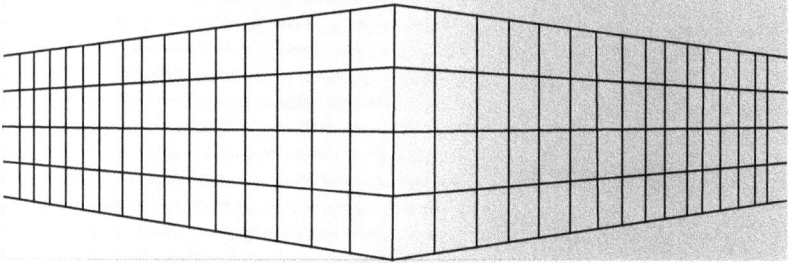

"Unpretentious and balanced operational thinking."

nal pursuit as a "chartable journey", (Figure 3-1).

And imagine that there are *three steering forces* that vie for precedence along the way:

1. *Valid Comprehension* – the interpretive reliability or ana-lytical soundness of the sponsor or "traveler".

2. *Corresponding Presumptions* – the expectations or pre-sumptive intensity of the sponsor or "traveler".

3. *Time* – Δt.

Each confronting the others with varying potency.

A *virtual* battleground of operational influences.

Now suppose that this battleground... any operational setting... is comprised of several principal elements.

Point A, the point of departure.

Case-specific yet all-inclusive, the context at Point A can vary in complexity from a simple frontline suggestion to a multifaceted strategic plan.

The fundamentals are identical.

And *Time* is solely relative.

A *Target Line* bears 45° from Point A to "operational infinity" (∞), and represents the basic objective.

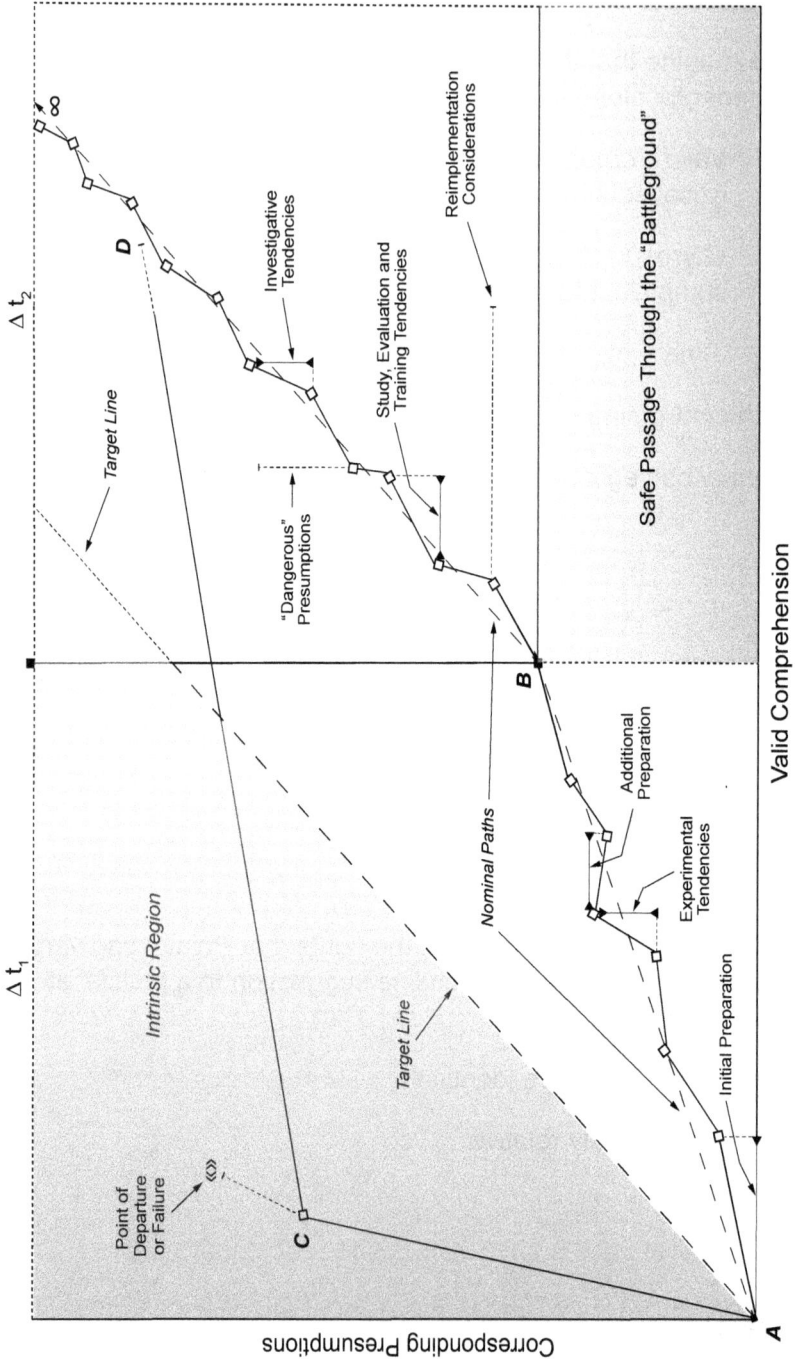

Figure 3-1

In other words, when departing Point A, the goal is to embark on a path that will *become parallel* to the Target Line.

This is the moment when *Valid Comprehension* (a rational grasp of circumstances and needs) and *Corresponding Presumptions* (theoretical expectations) are properly balanced.

Point B signifies this milestone, where the *Nominal Path* of the pursuit becomes parallel to the Target Line and Time inherently resets.

Moving forward from Point B, expectations are instinctively realistic, with enlightened simplicity in decision-making and planning.

Secure operational footing.

And sustainable prosperity.

The time to reach Point B... a critical *learning period*... demands an impartial evaluation of operational and functional characteristics.

But in an *aggressively patient* manner.

Nominal Path segments *(A→B) and (B→∞)*... shown as consecutive dashed lines... represent the *general* "mindset" for operational development in each segment.

And demonstrate sound intentions.

Actual "steps" taken along the nominal segments appear as

solid lines, each ending with a square "decision point".

The "approach angle" of each step depicts the underlying per-ception of the traveler as well as the likely inclination of func-tional responses.

Resulting interactions serve to alter the approach angle of subsequent steps at each decision point... in terms of presump-tions, valid comprehension and Δt... to reach or maintain a parallel reference to the Target Line.

Figure 3-1 is thus an elementary portrayal of an ultimately suc-cessful developmental journey.

Nominal segment (A→B) takes an initial heading, or "departure angle", of *less than* 45° from Point A.

Accordingly, the importance of "realistic awareness" (the level of *Valid Comprehension* along the "x" axis) significantly exceeds "presumptive expectations" (the *Corresponding Presumptions* along the "y" axis) in this early stage.

Nothing is selfishly nor baselessly presumed, and the *receptive capacity* of the operating environment is not forcibly typecast.

Suitable forethought, study and training are paramount.

"Preparation" and "Experimental Tendencies" are the primary considerations at decision points along the nominal (A→B) seg-ment, and are vital factors in early developmental contact.

Extrinsic *preparatory* interactions ("x" axis trends) will strengthen familiarity with the existing operational setting and enrich the *receptive capacity* of the operating environment.

A desire... or need... for extended *preparation* work will decrease the departure angle of nominal segment (A→B) and lengthen the *learning period* (the time to reach Point B).

But it will also have a valuable stabilizing effect, reducing operational friction and safeguarding an ultimate arrival at Point B.

The "patient" part of an *aggressively patient* stance.

By contrast, Experimental Tendencies ("y" axis trends) will carefully test certain presumptions that might not yet be warranted.

Such *extrinsically-based* initiatives could increase the approach angle of nominal segment (A→B) and provide a quicker trip to Point B (a *learning period* advantage), if successful.

The "aggressive" side of *aggressively patient*.

Beyond Point B... nominal segment (B→∞)... the path remains infinitely parallel to the Target Line.

Presumptions are well-substantiated.

Sustainably prosperous conditions.

To ensure stable yet innovative growth, certain decision-point inclinations dictate the approach angles of steps along nominal segment (B→∞), as well.

"Study, Evaluation and Training (SET) Tendencies" favor valid comprehension and unpretentious operational thinking in decision-making.

Each step verifying and confirming existing operational circumstances by measuring fundamental values in extrinsic terms.

Advocating a sound grasp of the operating environment, assuring continued functional strength and stability and preserving the principles of the Target Line.

"Investigative Tendencies" offer an opportunity to press capabilities and receptive capacities to reach new levels, within the realm of "extrinsic confidence".

But if the levels of comprehension or receptive capacity become uncertain or problematic, actual steps along the (B→∞) segment can revert to "Reimplementation Considerations" in which Preparation and early Experimental factors are re-examined.

"Dangerous Presumptions" implies a frame of mind that is far ahead of the curve... beyond the purpose and security of Investigative and SET Tendencies.

Here, expectations no longer reflect actual circumstances and begin to overtake capabilities.

Causes for this diversion... harmful functional influences... must be identified and reversed.

And the course returned to sustainability, within the assurances of appropriate Investigative and SET Tendencies.

Many endeavors, however, first trudge through the *Intrinsic Region...* line segment *(A→C)*. Here, at Point A, comprehension of operational circumstances is falsely assumed, and the departure angle is far too steep.

As a result, related efforts are accompanied by fabricated expectations that are not consistent with true operational capabilities and receptive capacities.

Prompted by inwardly focused and "privileged" speculation, they continuously impose non-realistic demands.

In-house or out-sourced "leaders" who promote these schemes are typically brimming with pre-conceived suppositions and constraints, but seldom wish (or attempt) to learn the true character of the operating environment. Ultimately perceived to have little credibility, they gain no respect or support.

Many times their intentions are unpleasantly belittled by the "masses", and pressing onward can become severely harmful.

Internal originators or out-sourced providers of this sort wander about fruitlessly in the Intrinsic Region.

Some learn the significance of outwardly focused fundamentals and seek a *pathway out*.

Most try to cope with the friction of repressed potential and unnecessarily low levels of performance by casting blame, convinced that things would be better (for them) "elsewhere".

Others simply disappear.

Hardly prosperous occurrences.

Line segment *(C→D)* depicts a "pathway out"; one that signals a profound change in focus from preconceived urges to valid comprehension. And relief from the harmful discord of the Intrinsic Region.

But prosperity has been notably impeded.

The intended two phases have become three: (A→C), (C→D) and *(D→∞)*. Point C now serves as the starting point, and Point D the belated Point B.

"Recovery time", Δt from Point C to Point D, reflects the time required to gain, or perhaps regain, trust and credibility.

The "time advantage", Δt from Point B to Point D, is the time gained by holding the proper convictions at Point A.

Though all decision points are characterized by an aggressively patient "pursuit of understanding", the Point C departure angle must *firmly* safeguard valid comprehension.

Preparation, Experimental, Investigative and SET Tendencies must be kept *well* within suitable approach angles.

In the end, when the "ultimate" course begins to make headway... toward *operational infinity* and parallel to the Target Line... no presumption will adversely conflict with the true nature of the operating environment.

And the receptive capacity of all participants will remain viable and free of friction.

All that is required... at any level, certainly, but best if driven broadly from the "top"... is a sincere willingness to first acquire, and then maintain, a sound grasp of operational traits.

One that is respectful, and not influenced by personal, political, privileged or bottom line *intrinsic* objectives.

Sustainable prosperity.

So, the journey awaits.

A humble suggestion or a bold strategic plan, there is no imaginative difference.

Promotional credibility and the utmost success at either level are secured by the same *extrinsic reasoning* mindset.

An *outwardly focused*... and wholly captivating... thought process that becomes the basis for all considerations.

Start selflessly.

Study.

Prepare.

Experiment.

Strive to reach... and maintain... a "parallel" condition in the *battleground of operational influences*.

Then stay within the assurances of acceptable decision-point tendencies.

Recognize *dangerous presumptions*.

If perceptions become clouded, *reimplement* and recover.

It's just that simple.

It costs nothing.

And in the words of Albert Einstein: "…the rest are details".

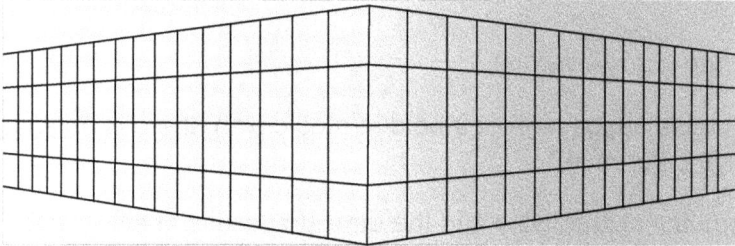

"And in the words of Albert Einstein: '...the rest are details'."

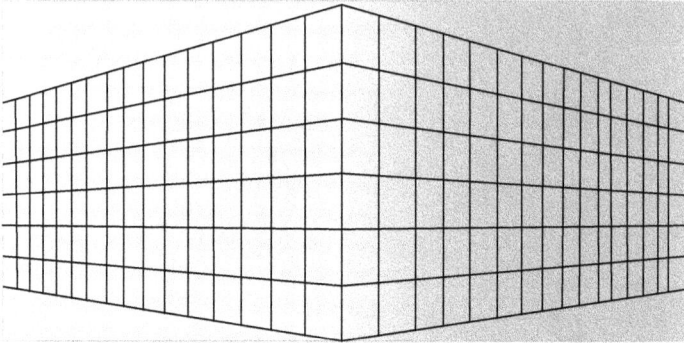

"...heightened enthusiasm... will fuel the evolution of positive, self-policing trends."

Chapter 4.

In Practice

Relevant to both *internal and external* functions, one must:

- Form a selfless perception of the operational setting.

- Pursue advancements that stay within the *acceptable decision-point tendencies* of *Chapter 3.*

- Properly accommodate the *steering forces* that vie for precedence.

Through an ongoing practice of study and contact, and a fair-minded assessment of feedback and criticism.

This commitment will stimulate constructive behavior at all levels, to the furthest extent of the operating environment.

Always-improving *receptive capacities* and a heightened enthusiasm for cooperative response will fuel the evolution of positive, *self-policing trends.*

Baseless presumptions will not eclipse the true functional characteristics of an operation; preconceived notions, conjecture or any sense of entitlement or privilege will not be given superior advantage.

The groundwork for sustainable prosperity.

Selected "Cases in Point".

Internal Areas of Operation –

Assume, for purposes here, that "internal operations" include the following in-house functions:

- Internal customer relationships... functional capacities or tasks that exist within an extended operation but outside a specific operating environment.

- The deeds and responsibilities of out-sourced service providers.

In any internal operational setting, competitive *domains* naturally exist.

If they are permitted to become dissociated "fortresses" however, they can be profoundly detrimental.

In this instance, each will grow to be defensive, often to a point of rash insensitivity to the general consequences of certain actions or responses.

Adjacent domains (*internal customers*) or out-sourced service providers become guiltless targets of blame for lapses, shortcomings or systemic failures.

And discussions are relegated to heated accusations or the "one-sided" nature of programs, rather than cooperative, forward-driven solutions.

Similarly, without a cooperative means of informed involvement, *individuals* will classically misjudge the intent of a plan, or will find it perplexing at best, regardless of their allegiance.

They will subsequently concede to the forceful "filtering" influences of inwardly focused colleagues or coworkers.

And the rationale of any proposal becomes distorted.

Consequently, internal customer "relationships" are habitually stressed and service provider participation is degraded.

An *extrinsic* mindset will counteract these situations by encouraging a *cooperative organizational approach*, and *resourceful methods* of exchanging information.

Job functions will evolve as one, and not be "led astray" by adjacent "domains", biased coworkers or uninformed overseers.

Suitably timed decisions will be made correctly with no attempt to force a specified outcome.

Sound operational strategies will be coactively developed internally, taking into account the proper insertion of outside service providers.

Value, in excess of any pre-determinable measure.

External Areas of Operation –

Now also assume that "external operations" include the following client and customer-side pursuits:

- Marketing and sales functions.

- Product support activities.

- Related administrative and transactional processes.

- Surveys, data collection, data management and associated activities.

Fueled by an eagerness to meet sales objectives, *competitive internal factions* can surface *externally* as well.

Yet they often reveal themselves as detached, contradictory, and sometimes self-promoting territorial pursuits.

Functionally disjointed and mutually exclusive, they can force outsiders to "take sides".

Likewise, from time to time, *independent "crusades"* are embarked upon by internal staff members... with good intentions... who feel duty-bound to resolve product support difficulties, but have no collaborative mechanism available to them.

Without an essential grasp of the "big picture", such efforts can be poorly cohesive and subject to fierce setbacks.

Localized promotional campaigns are a common theme of short-range external strategies.

Still, these *transitory* forms of customer contact... focused or point-of-sale pursuits with fixed, often hurried end points... are seldom designed to favor external inclinations.

Pressured by sharply defined performance measures that entirely favor internal objectives... inventory reduction, quotas, in-house competition and the like; or superficial "specials" meant to promptly remedy failing market penetration or to retrieve a lost account... they too can become self-defeating.

Nonetheless, they are often the *only* marketplace tactics in use.

Compartmentalized and inconsistent, they frequently reflect an inward bias that weakens the cooperative nature of each contact, and at times implies a crude deficiency in "industry awareness".

Perhaps most annoyed are disheartened former customers who have been newly targeted for retrieval. Offhand "specials" that *still* lack a grasp of what is particularly relevant can merely serve as unfriendly reminders of past frustrations.

"Arduous" *questionnaires* are used at times to sound out customer needs.

Assuming that a contact person will gratuitously suggest a product application, propose an administrative approach or provide generic qualifying factors suddenly upon request could frankly be considered naive.

The burden of this research should not fall on the shoulders of customers or market acquaintances.

On a broader scale, *prescriptive external campaigns* are occasionally devised by distant control centers to fulfill common needs... product line introductions, program launches, rebate schemes, corporate image enhancement and so forth.

Pre-conceived, longer term and largely presumptive, they are often comprised of ill-considered strategies that are puzzling to regional interests.

With rigid operating criteria and internally-based measures of success, they attempt to impose "Company" frames of reference on local practices.

Out of touch with "resident" cultures, needs and applications, these campaigns can be frustratingly irrelevant.

Again, *extrinsic conduct* will correct these faults by advocating certain underlying practices that will build genuine "inside-outside" cohesiveness. *More specifically...*

Acquire and *maintain* an attentive grasp of the market(s), especially the *fundamental challenges* that marketplace contacts commonly face.

Then, learn the *language* and *patterns of operation*, the ups and downs; busy times, slow periods.

In turn, provide methods to assemble thoughts and ideas *internally* through a broadly accessible mechanism.

One that encourages *cooperative* involvement from the *furthest extent* of the operating environment, making it easier to control the scope of *competitive internal factions* and eliminating the need for *independent "crusades"*.

Within this context, determine what might already be known about a "target opportunity" using in-house data from historical encounters... information that can provide a factual understanding of *necessary* product or service applications.

Correlate these internal thoughts, ideas and in-house data with the *fundamental challenges* and the *patterns of operation* that have been identified, accompanied by a fluent awareness of the resident *language and terminology*.

Decide how best to interact during downturns, slumps or slow periods, and how to be efficiently supportive in busy times as well.

And determine how helpful information can be *tactfully* gained from every *new* experience, without the use of burdensome *questionnaires*, to improve future endeavors.

Finally, establish internal operating criteria that will require *all external pursuits*, throughout the organization, to adhere to the protocol and make proper use of available information.

The outwardly focused perspective instilled by this "code of be-havior" will enhance the potential to *rebuild lost affiliations*, and provide opportunities for *transitory encounters* to mature into complex relationships.

Prescriptive campaigns from distant sources will be adapted to become locally relevant; marketplace considerations will be free of artificial influences.

Product sales will flow naturally. Sound applications will emerge, and often result in unforeseen opportunities.

No longer the driving force, internally-focused goals will be viewed as limiting factors... and revenues will exceed what could possibly have been projected, at lower cost.

In practice, as these examples suggest, a higher level of "real-ization" is of critical importance.

An appreciation that makes possible a *valid comprehension* of the internal and external areas of operation.

Allowing common sense to govern every functional setting.

Customers, internal staff, colleagues and associates will be comfortable for the long term.

The true measure of success.

"Extrinsic reasoning... 'outwardly focused thinking' ... is the key dynamic."

Chapter 5.

The Key Dynamic

Extrinsic reasoning... outwardly focused thinking... is the key dynamic.

If understood and faithfully practiced, it will deliver the highest level of operational success.

It will add pivotal value at any station, and is fundamentally essential to both *internal* and *external* areas of operation.

It will provide the greatest likelihood of sustained prosperity; vigorous in principle yet unpretentious in nature.

Remarkably simple and immediately available.

And, again, it *costs nothing.*

It requires only that *decision point sentiments* not be predetermined during the course of *Chapter 3's "formative journey",* even in long-established operational settings. Instead they must properly accommodate the *three steering forces.*

Revenue targets, budgeting thresholds, fiscal forecasting techniques and similar "reckoning tools", when used to judge tactical merits, unfortunately *impose rigid decision-making guidelines* that work against this concept. Devised to bring about a particular outcome, they essentially become a hindrance.

Organizational tendencies should rather support the possibility of *various "futures"*, with one being likely as another to occur... particularly those that differ from pre-conceived notions or inwardly focused agendas.

Extrinsic reasoning is the interpretive mechanism that *best engages the steering forces* as they compete.

A broader mental model that correctly perceives operational characteristics and shapes observations.

Enabling *Valid Comprehension* and *Corresponding Presumptions* to reach parity at the earliest moment... and offering safe passage to the *brightest* "future".

Extrinsic reasoning. Outwardly focused thinking.

The key dynamic.

"...support the possibility of various "futures"... particularly those that differ from pre-conceived notions..."

Chapter 6.

The Ultimate Challenge

A cultural transformation must take place.

Giving way to extrinsic reasoning as the *key dynamic*, with the condition that it must underlie operational initiatives and text-book methods, and exemplify "leadership" and "vision".

Rousing an "extrinsic" awareness in everyone; each person making the point by personal example.

And gauged by the pervasiveness of outwardly focused thought.

But it will take time.

Early on, fundamental changes will contend with an inordinate surge of "urgent" troubles.

Many result from newly available lines of communication that are besieged with pent-up concerns.

Some are caused by necessary decisions that must be made prematurely with limited, or not yet substantiated, obtainable information.

Clearly in this "maiden" phase, the need to manage frustration is imperative.

But with an *outwardly focused* eye on the horizon, there will be a feeling of secure simplicity in meeting all challenges, knowing that a *defining moment* is comfortably at hand.

Operational volatility will calm with the cooperative understanding that further ahead, any uneasiness will be absorbed into a fair, equitable and stimulating developmental sequence.

And the resulting organizational strength and operating efficiency will produce, in due course, a soundly functional framework on a solid foundation.

The advent of sustainable prosperity.

"Extrinsic reasoning... outwardly focused thinking... is the key dynamic."

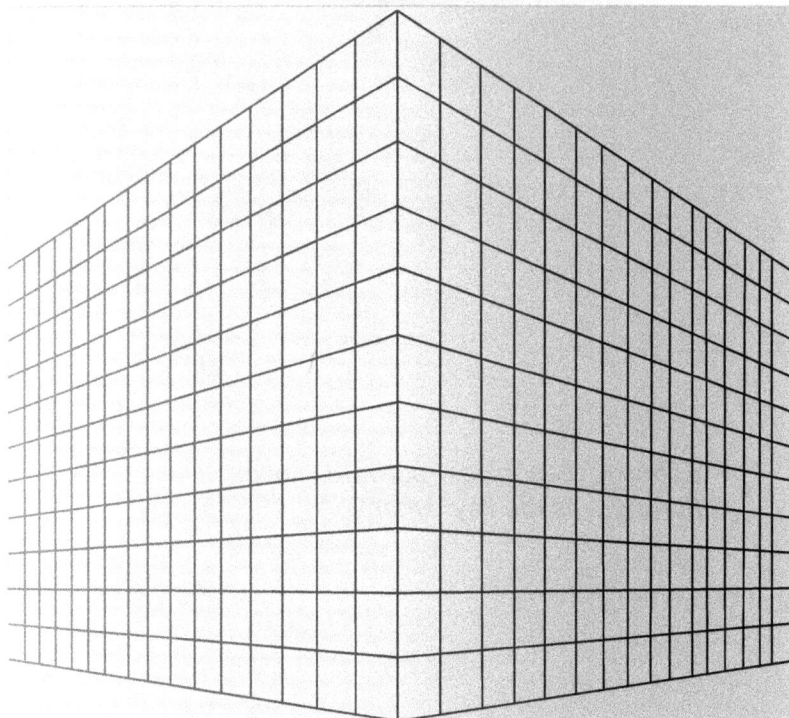

"...with an outwardly focused eye on the horizon, there will be a feeling of secure simplicity in meeting all challenges..."

"A Defining Moment... The Advent of Sustainable Prosperity" offers a candid reminder of the basics....

...or perhaps a needed **introduction** to them.

Through this undemanding *"overview"*, T. Lewis Company, *www.tlewiscompany.com*, recounts the importance of a fundamental rule of operational behavior.

One that strengthens functional principles, capabilities and receptive capacities, and provides a pathway to sustainable prosperity for small businesses.

A simple form of thought that allows unrecognized advantages and untapped internal resources to emerge, often intensely critical to smaller operations.

Practiced and unpretentious, risk-free and highly effective, *this "introductory abstract" sets the stage for a classically sustainable journey.*

It is the true starting point.

Notes and Observations...